MJF BOOKS | New York

201
weird true facts

WTF

[psychology]

harry bright &
jakob anser

illustrations by
tang yau hoong

Published by MJF Books
Fine Communications
322 Eighth Avenue
New York, NY 10001

WTF *[psychology]*
LC Control Number: 2016905190
ISBN 978-1-60671-349-5

Printed in the United States of America.

Designed by Lisa Chovnick
Illustrations by Tang Yau Hoong

MJF Books and the MJF colophon are trademarks
of Fine Creative Media, Inc.

QF 10 9 8 7 6 5 4 3 2 1

201
weird true facts

WTF

[psychology]

Written around 1600 B.C., the Edwin Smith Surgical Papyrus, named after the American archaeologist who purchased the scroll in Egypt in 1862, is the earliest extant document to describe the brain. The papyrus outlines treatments for 48 medical traumas—everything from dislocations to open wounds to head injuries.

Case six of the Edwin Smith Surgical Papyrus details a gaping head wound and notes that the brain looks like "those corrugations which form in molten copper." This likely refers to the sulci and gyri, the furrows and ridges along the brain's surface. Ancient Egyptian doctors could describe the brain, but they didn't understand or value its function. They believed the heart was the center of emotions, thought, and personality, as well as the home of the soul. When mummifying pharaohs, embalmers punched a hole in the braincase by jamming a rod up the nose, then emptied the skull of all brain matter.

MULTITASKING WAS NEVER A THING.
Lin Xie, a sixth-century Confucian scholar, is
believed to have conducted one of the first
psychology experiments when he asked his
students to simultaneously draw a circle with
one hand and a square with the other. They
demonstrated that trying to do two things at
once often means neither is done correctly.

German physician Wilhelm Wundt was the
first person to refer to himself as a psychologist.
Before 1879, when Wundt established the first
formal experimental psychology lab, at the
University of Leipzig, psychology had been
considered a subdiscipline of biology and
philosophy.

THE FRONTAL LOBE IS WHERE THE PUN HAPPENS.

Witzelsucht is a rare neurological condition
that gets its name from the German *witzeln*,
meaning "to wisecrack," and *Sucht*, meaning
"addiction." This jones for joking is caused by
damage to the brain's frontal lobe, the part
responsible for decision-making, planning, and
judgment. So while they don't understand or
laugh at other people's humor, wisenheimers
with this condition go giddy at their own
uncontrollable barrages of bad puns.

According to psychology professor Robert Provine, "There was laughter long before there was humor." Laughter actually evolved as a social cue to let others know we feel good about them. In his study "Laughing, Tickling, and the Evolution of Speech and Self," Provine found that only 10 to 15 percent of the statements preceding a laugh were funny, and nearly half of conversational laughter comes from a speaker laughing at herself.

People born deaf punctuate their signing with laughter at the exact same points in conversation that hearing people do when speaking. Which means the comment "I have to take my cat to the vet now, haha" is as commonplace as it is illogical.

In a 2015 study published in *Computers in Human Behavior,* a journal exploring computer use from a psychological perspective, researchers wondered who watches online cat videos, why, and to what effect? A survey of nearly 7,000 internet users showed that consuming kitty content boosts mood and energy. Participants pounced on the opportunity to watch feline footage at work, but they didn't feel guilty because the positive procrastination left them refreshed and ready to tackle tough assignments.

What's a great way to recharge your batteries? Laugh. When subjects in an Australian study were given a boring task to perform, then shown clips of the British sitcom *Mr. Bean,* they worked twice as long as those who had watched nature or business management videos.

According to Michael Graziano, author of *Consciousness and the Social Brain,* social behaviors such as smiling and laughing evolved out of defensive responses to aggression. Smiling started as a counter to another's baring of teeth, while laughter developed as a "touché signal" during rough play. You can see this when a mother tickles her child: The mother mocks an aggressive posture; the child smiles in response. As the mother moves in, the child laughs *before* she is touched—a reaction to the trespass against her personal space. It's a social cue to the aggressor that says, "Hey, I'm cute, don't kill me."

Many creatures wail in distress, and even crocodiles produce tears, but only humans combine the two into the social behavior of emotional crying. Michael Graziano argues that crying evolved because our ancestors liked to punch one another in the face to solve problems. Tears and alarm calls emerged as distress signals designed to elicit comfort and social reunion. Ad Vingerhoets, author of *Why Only Humans Weep*, argues that crying helps us survive the prolonged childhood intrinsic to our species.

I CAN'T SMILE WITHOUT YOU. Women who get Botox injections to treat crow's feet may become depressed afterward. The shots freeze the muscles around the eyes and disrupt their contractions during a natural smile. In the 19th century, French neurologist G. B. Duchenne de Boulogne noticed that a cold, faked smile was often limited to the mouth, and studies have shown that smiles not involving the eyes were perceived as fake—by both the recipient *and* the person smiling.

Women who get Botox injections to correct frown lines often report feeling happier after the treatment. Facial expressions affect our emotional state. We smile when we're happy, but smiling also *makes* us happy.

If you're unhappy, there's good news: It won't kill you. A 2015 study published in *The Lancet* analyzed more than 700,000 medical records from the U.K. Million Women Study and reported that unhappy women had the same overall death rate as happy ones. The best way to be happy is to stay healthy, because, as researchers point out, illness is the biggest cause of unhappiness.

IS THE GLASS HALF EMPTY OR HALF FULL? That may depend on your genes. A study published in *Psychological Science* in 2013 showed that some people are genetically predisposed to see the world in a negative light.

There's a direct link between time spent on Facebook and depressive symptoms. A 2015 study published in the *Journal of Social and Clinical Psychology* found that when we make social comparisons between our mundane lives and the "highlight reel" of our friends' lives, we feel worse about ourselves. In another study, conducted by Copenhagen's Happiness Research Institute, participants who quit Facebook cold turkey for a week reported feeling happier, more decisive, less lonely, and more satisfied overall with their social lives.

Our brains have a distorted body image. They devote more space to controlling our hands, tongue, genitals, and facial features than our limbs. Pioneering neurosurgeon Wilder Penfield discovered this in the 1930s while performing brain surgeries—on conscious patients. Penfield's homunculus is a grotesque illustration showing the size of each body part proportional to its cortical representation and sensitivity.

———

Nearly 80 percent of amputees feel pain in a phantom limb. In fact, if you had arthritis in your arm, you might not only feel the lost arm after amputation, you'd feel the arthritis pain, too.

To **test** the "rubber hand illusion," subjects with normal brains are tricked into believing a rubber hand is part of their bodies. Researchers place a rubber hand in a participant's field of vision and position her real hand just out of sight. The real and fake hands are stroked simultaneously, and the subject's brain quickly adopts the fake one as its own. The effect is so powerful that when researchers threaten the rubber hand with a hammer, participants recoil in fear of getting hurt.

THAT'S HEAVY, MAN. We often refer to important ideas as heavy and frivolous ideas as lightweight. Turns out our bodies can influence our thinking simply by holding a lighter or heavier object. Participants in a study published in *Psychological Science* were given either a heavy or light clipboard, then were asked to consider a hypothetical problem of injustice. Those with heavy clipboards thought more deeply, while those with light ones gave the problem less consideration.

When you first looked at the cover of this book, did you see a bird or a gramophone? The illustration, called "Songbird," employs negative space (a blank field around a primary subject) to form two competing interpretations of visual information. You can't see both at once, because your eyes jump from one to the other in an attempt to avoid uncertainty. Images with multiple interpretations are called multistable.

———

Corporate logos often cleverly exploit negative space. From NBC's famous peacock to the Hartford Whalers emblem to the hidden arrow in the FedEx logo, multistable designs effectively reward our brains. Once we see the secret shape, we feel included in a discerning group.

Apple has sold more than a billion devices and has one of the most ubiquitous logos on the planet. But could you draw it from memory? Is the bottom of the apple curved or flat? Does the stem lean to the left or the right? Is a bite taken out of it? How big? On which side? A recent study showed that less than one percent of test subjects could draw Apple's logo perfectly, even though nearly all participants thought they could. One reason? Attentional saturation. When our brains see something over and over, they learn that its details are unimportant.

The charismatic power Apple founder Steve Jobs held over his developers has been described as a "reality distortion field," a term originating from a *Star Trek* episode featuring aliens who project mass illusions to create virtual realities.

Jerks are remarkably adept at selling their ideas. Although not necessarily more creative than anybody else, jerks, according to a study, tend to win the day the more "argumentative, egotistical, aggressive, headstrong, and hostile" they are.

Organizations centered around a charismatic leader often demonstrate a "routinization of charisma" that turns the leader's beliefs into a system of rules and laws. Ergo, Christ becomes Christianity. Political regimes whose outgoing leader's beliefs have not been sufficiently routinized and that lack a charismatic heir apparent usually fail.

Gaslighting **is** a form of mental abuse in which someone attempts to destroy or radically alter another person's perception of reality. The name comes from Patrick Hamilton's 1938 play *Gas Light*, about a man's systematic attempts to convince his wife she's insane. He repeatedly turns down their home's gaslight and pretends to be puzzled whenever his wife wonders why it's so dim.

MOODS ARE
AS CONTAGIOUS
AS GERMS.

201 weird true facts

"**E**motional contagion" starts with
unconscious mimicry (you smiled, so now I'm
smiling). Then comes internal feedback (I
smiled, so I feel happy). Finally, the infected
synchronize with the people around them (gee,
isn't being happy great?). Be careful, though: It's
just as easy to catch a sad bug. In her 2002 study
"The Ripple Effect: Emotional Contagion and
Its Influence on Group Behavior," Sigal Barsade
describes people as "walking mood inductors,"
influencing—and being influenced by—the
moods of others.

Timothie **Bright's** *Treatise of Melancholie,*
published in 1586, is the first comprehensive
description of depression in English. A physician
and clergyman, Bright details several symptoms
of melancholy, such as nightmares, false
laughter, and witnessing fantastical apparitions.
He advises that melancholic temperaments
would improve in thin air from the "South
and South-East." Many scholars
believe Shakespeare used Bright's
treatise to flesh out his most
famous depressive, Hamlet,
who claims, "I am but mad
north-north-west. When the
wind is southerly, I know a
hawk from a handsaw."

Just being at risk for severe depression ages you. A 2014 paper in *Molecular Psychiatry* showed that healthy girls between the ages of 10 and 14 whose mothers had a history of depression had shorter telomeres than their lower-risk peers. Telomeres are the caps at the end of our chromosomes; they naturally shorten over time, so their length is like a biological clock. Even though they'd never been diagnosed with depression, the at-risk girls had telomere lengths equivalent to someone six years older.

———

Owning just one guinea pig is illegal in Switzerland, because these herd animals are prone to loneliness.

Loneliness **may** reduce life expectancy as much as smoking 15 cigarettes a day. A recent meta-analysis of 70 studies revealed that even people who live alone and think of themselves as happy have a higher mortality risk than those living with other people.

Anthropologist and evolutionary psychologist Robin Dunbar has hypothesized that living in complex social groups leads to increased relative brain size and problem-solving ability among vertebrates. For some unknown reason, Dunbar's social brain hypothesis does not apply to carnivores.

In a 2006 study called "The Effect of Meat Consumption on Body Odor Attractiveness," male participants ate a meat diet for a month, then switched to vegetarian meals. Pads worn in their armpits for the last 24 hours of each diet were presented to female participants. The women strongly preferred the smell of the vegetarians, classifying their odor as "more attractive, more pleasant, and less intense."

Three recent experiments sought to determine what kinds of men prefer women with large breasts. The first pointed to men from lower socioeconomic backgrounds, the second to men who want to have children, and the third to men who were simply hungry.

In a study of nearly 10,000 people, men with demanding partners were two and a half times more likely to die within the next 10 years than those in less stressful relationships.

———

Women, however, proved immune to nagging.

———

When you get into an argument with your boyfriend and he starts complaining about *how* you argue, he is switchtracking. The name comes by way of the railroad, where trains can be diverted onto different tracks at the throw of a switch. Someone who feels threatened will often switchtrack to send the conversation in a direction where they are more confident.

Male novelists idealize romantic love differently than female novelists do. While male novelists tend to locate romantic allure in a sense of mystery and the ineffable, female novelists place a premium on conversation and intellectual parity.

———

The most incredible thing humans do? Have conversations. Across cultures, people converse as if they're playing Ping-Pong; on average, each turn lasts around two seconds. The typical gap between turns is 200 milliseconds—about the time it takes to say one syllable. This is possible because we plan responses well before our interlocutor has finished speaking.

———

The average conversational gap in Japan? *Seven* milliseconds.

According to decluttering guru Marie Kondo, author of the best seller *The Life-Changing Magic of Tidying Up*, the mental and physical toll of keeping an unused item is greater than the cost of throwing it out.

ONCE A LIGHT BONUS, NOW A DAILY BURDEN. People check their email an average of 77 times per day, UC Irvine professor of informatics Gloria Mark has found. "The more email people do," she says, "the lower is their assessed productivity [and] mood at the end of the day."

Email has become an "approach-avoid conflict," psychologist Larry Rosen explains. "We know there might be a gem in [our inbox] somewhere right now, but we have to sift through all the crap to find it." That's because email's accessibility and its unpredictable pleasures stimulate our brain's seeking circuits, which are mediated by the dopamine that rewards us every time we find something important.

According to a 2014 study, productivity is proportional to time worked—but only up to 49 hours per week. People who put in 70 hours had the same productivity as those who worked 56 hours.

Researchers from the University of Michigan found that taking a daytime nap counteracts impulsive behavior and boosts tolerance for frustration.

———

The amygdala, a primitive part of the brain, is responsible for "fight or flight" responses. When we're at work, four factors can force us out of a reflective mode and into a reactive, more primitive one: getting insufficient rest, not feeling valued or respected, lacking the freedom to focus on the highest priorities, and being disconnected from any mission greater than ourselves.

ONE ALPHA DOG PER PACK. In a series of experiments conducted at UC Berkeley's Haas School of Business, leaders consistently under-performed when grouped together. Teams of powerful people were the least productive in part because, instead of focusing on the work, they argued about who should have higher status.

In a leadership study commonly referred to as the "Cookie Monster experiment," researchers grouped people into teams of three, asking two members to write a social policy paper and the third to evaluate the work. After half an hour, researchers brought in a plate of five cookies, enough for each participant to have one treat, but not two. The "bosses" not only took seconds, but devoured the snacks à la *Sesame Street*'s Cookie Monster, munching with their mouths open and scattering crumbs everywhere.

Harvard **Business School** professor Amy Edmondson has found that a team's creativity, productivity, and success come not from the star talents of its individual members as much as from its group culture—especially if it includes what she calls "psychological safety." According to Edmondson, psychological safety "describes a team climate characterized by interpersonal trust and mutual respect, in which people are comfortable being themselves."

In his book *Outliers,* Malcolm Gladwell summarizes the psychological research of Anders Ericsson and introduces into popular culture the idea that it takes 10,000 hours of deliberate practice to become an expert at anything. This isn't necessarily the case. Ericsson himself claims he never said how many hours it takes. Further, a meta-analysis by psychologist Brooke Macnamara demonstrated that practice accounts for 26 percent of achievement variation in cerebral games such as chess, 21 percent in playing a musical instrument, and only 18 percent in sports. Virtuosity depends on a mix of psychological, biological, environmental, and health factors, combined with good old-fashioned practice.

How can a pro golfer at Augusta suddenly lose his swing on the back nine? Choking is a cruel by-product of the stress of competition and the glare of the spotlight. When we're first taught the mechanics of hitting a nine iron, for example, we store that information using explicit memory, which allows us to describe and analyze our experience. But once we absorb the lesson and start playing more freely, we operate on implicit, procedural memory—what athletes call muscle memory. Under extreme stress, athletes may overthink the physical process and inadvertently trigger their explicit memory. The end result: discombobulation.

NATURE OR NURTURE? Biological approaches purport that nearly all behavior is inherited and has an adaptive, evolutionary function. But what if nurture is the next generation's nature? Studies have shown that people born with no musical proclivities but who nonetheless spend their lives practicing bore children with native musical talent. In other words, years of practice change your nature down to the DNA level.

Studies of twins have proved that genes are the primary determinant of many personality traits, as well as IQ. The Minnesota Study of Twins Reared Apart, a multidecade study that followed identical and fraternal twins separated at an early age, established that leadership and an affinity for traditional values are both inherited. A more recent twin study, published in *The Leadership Quarterly* in 2013, identified rs4950 as the genetic marker for passing leadership ability to later generations.

Though reared apart, the so-called Jim twins led astonishingly parallel lives. Both were named Jim by their adoptive parents, did well in math but poorly in spelling, suffered from tension headaches as teenagers, divorced women named Linda, married women named Betty, named their first-born son James Alan (although one spelled it with two *l*s), had an adopted brother named Larry, named their dogs Toy, worked as part-time law enforcement officers, drank Miller Lite beer, smoked Salem cigarettes, and built woodworking shops in their garages. At one point, each Jim drove a light-blue Chevrolet to vacation on the same three-block strip of Florida beach. They were separated at four weeks and didn't meet again until they were 39 years old.

Identical twins don't agree on what's attractive.

———

I'LL TAKE THE USUAL. Multiple studies have indicated that we're most attracted to average-looking, symmetrical faces. "Attractive Faces Are Only Average," a landmark study published in *Psychological Science,* showed that composite images assembled from multiple faces were judged more attractive than individuals' faces. Psychologists believe this is due to koinophilia, a term derived from the Greek *koinos,* meaning "the usual," and *philos,* meaning "fondness." The evolutionary hypothesis is that we prefer partners with average features because those on the extremes may contain mutations.

In 2006 a team of Israeli scientists developed software to perform "digital face beautification"—essentially they can scan someone's face, and the software will enhance its symmetry and correct any "bugs" to make it scientifically more beautiful. When they ran James Franco's mug, nothing happened.

In a 2012 study, men and women tried on different wigs to determine hair color's effect on courtship. Perhaps unsurprisingly, men approached the women wearing blond wigs more frequently than they did their raven-haired counterparts. (Previous studies had shown that blond women also receive more money when fund-raising door-to-door and get more tips when waitressing.) Women, however, did not return the sentiment. Blond men struck out just as frequently as brown-haired men.

Men and women did agree on one thing: Gingers are best avoided.

Redheads are twice as likely to avoid the dentist. The reason? They're significantly more sensitive to pain and require 20 percent more anesthetic to reach an optimum dose. Light skin and freckles come from a mutation to the MC1R gene, which influences pain sensitivity and—in most people, anyway—turns red pigments to brown.

NOT ALL PLACEBO PILLS ARE CREATED EQUAL. Expensive sugar pills, for example, have been shown to possess greater analgesic effects than cheap ones.

Your body has two systems for understanding pain. One is sensory, related to the type and magnitude of the stimulus: Did I stub my toe or cut myself with a chain saw? The other is an emotional system that determines how you feel about the pain and is influenced by such factors as your past history with the stimulus. This means you can minimize pain with positive emotions or intensify it with negative ones.

———

Your brain treats the pain of social rejection the same way it treats physical pain—which is why studies proved acetaminophen dulls both kinds.

Mindfulness meditation reduces pain more effectively than either a placebo or "sham mindfulness," as researchers called the phony breathing techniques they taught one group of participants. Their 2015 study, published in *The Journal of Neuroscience,* is the first to distinguish mindfulness meditation as mechanistically different from other pain relievers. Mindfulness activates neural regions related to thinking and emotion, whereas placebos work by deactivating regions related to sensation.

Mindfulness-based stress reduction and cognitive therapy have been shown to alleviate mental distress suffered by patients with cancer, cardiovascular disease, chronic pain, depression, and anxiety, as well as improve their quality of life. In healthy adults and children, mindfulness has been shown to *prevent* anxiety and depression.

———

Many psychologists now believe being mindful can slow one's perception of time.

Are you even listening to me?

A 2015 study published in *The Journal of Neuroscience* offers proof that we suffer from "inattentional deafness" when up to our eyes in smartphone stimulation. You have limits on the amount of stimuli you can perceive, so a lot of visuals—new high score! viral video!—reduce your ability to process unattended sounds, such as, say, your spouse's voice.

The **internet's** near-unlimited access to information has ushered in the first global economy driven by psychology. As writer Mark Manson argues, for most of human existence, land (and thus food) was the primary economic scarcity. But with the advent of the Industrial Revolution, we needed less land and more workers to operate machines, so labor became society's organizing principle. In the 20th century, finding ourselves with plenty of food *and* goods, we needed information and the media to tell us what to buy. We now have more information and media than we can possibly consume, so the primary economic driver is attention.

In a 2015 study by the Pew Research Center, 89 percent of participating cell phone owners said they had used these devices during their most recent social gathering. While children believed multitasking to be a skill, 82 percent of adults felt it had harmed their social interactions.

———————

The creators and marketers of the Lumosity "brain training" program agreed in 2016 to pay $2 million to the Federal Trade Commission, which had accused the company of deceiving consumers into believing its games could help them perform better at work and in school, as well as reduce cognitive impairment associated with serious health conditions and aging.

People suffering from Capgras syndrome become convinced that an imposter has replaced someone close to them.

In 2016, Harvard neurologists R. Ryan Darby and David Caplan coined the term *Cat-gras syndrome,* in reference to a man who believed his cat was an entirely different cat.

In 2013 a Dutch researcher was able to find only 56 documented historical cases of clinical zoanthropy, a rare delusion whose sufferers believe they're animals. Boanthropy, a subset of zoanthropy, is an even rarer disorder, in which a person believes he's a cow or an ox. An exemplar of boanthropy is Nebuchadnezzar II, king of the Neo-Babylonian Empire, who sent the Jews into exile. According to the Bible (Daniel 4:33), he was "driven from men and did eat grass as oxen."

———

Jerusalem syndrome is a phenomenon whereby a seemingly stable person becomes psychotic after arriving in Jerusalem. The afflicted are known to have become obsessed with personal hygiene, worn ankle-length gowns they fashioned from bedsheets, and shouted psalms and extemporized sermons at the city's holy sites.

In **"Jerusalem,"** a short story from Neil Gaiman's collection *Trigger Warning,* a British woman on holiday is stricken with Jerusalem syndrome. A trigger warning cautions that a piece of content—such as an article, book, or film—contains material that may remind audiences of past traumas. These warnings have themselves triggered controversy in academia. Professors have described trigger warnings as everything from "sound pedagogy" to a "form of narcissism" to emblems of a "culture of avoidance."

Clinical psychologist George Bonanno has adopted the term *potentially traumatic event* to propose that an incident is not traumatic until someone experiences it as such.

Whether you think an event is traumatic may depend on your resilience, which, according to developmental psychologist Norman Garmezy, can be difficult to study because it emerges only in the face of obstacles. In other words, your resilience cannot be proved if you've never been challenged.

WHAT'S YOUR GLITCH? Déjà vu, from the French meaning "already seen," denotes an overwhelming feeling that you've experienced a particular moment before, even though common sense tells you otherwise. Neuroscientists believe it kicks in when your brain recognizes a familiar pattern and erratically overlays a past memory onto your current situation. Interestingly, part of déjà vu is knowing the experience is impossible. It's your brain's way of saying, "Oops, never mind."

A **2014 entry** in the *Journal of Medical Case Reports* tells the strange story of a 23-year-old British man who was stuck in a loop of chronic déjà vu for *eight years*. He described going for a haircut and having a feeling of déjà vu—then having déjà vu of feeling déjà vu! He likened his experience to being trapped in the supernatural psychological movie *Donnie Darko*.

Hyperthymesia, from the Greek *hyper,*
meaning "excessive," and *thymesis,* meaning
"remembering," signifies a rare condition
granting people the ability to recall their lives
in encyclopedic detail—not only where they
were on a specific day, but what they ate for
breakfast that morning, what song they heard
on the radio, etc. There are so few cases that
the mechanisms behind this uncanny recall are
little understood, but we know that even
people with total autobiographical recall also
have imperfect, "false" memories. The irony is
that they nonetheless retrieve amazing
amounts of accurate detail using the same
process as the rest of us.

Our **memories** aren't like fixed photographs stored in the cloud. They're webs of sensory inputs that, when linked together, tell a story. And that story changes over time. Whenever we recall a memory, we embellish and revise it, we attach our present emotional state, and we save the edited version as the "true" memory. Rather than a storehouse of information about your past, your memory is actually a reflection of who you are now.

Neuroscientists at the Salk Institute for Biological Studies recently reported that the brain's memory capacity is 10 times greater than formerly thought. They believe it's no smaller than a petabyte, roughly equivalent to four times the information stored in the U.S. Library of Congress.

Have you ever walked from one room to another to retrieve an object, then forgotten what you were looking for? Don't worry, you're not losing your mind. Called the "location updating effect" or "doorway effect," this common memory lapse occurs as the brain tries to take in details of its new surroundings. Since the brain records in segments rather than continuously, it throws up a mental partition between our experiences of the two rooms. That wall disrupts the connections composing our memory, so remembering anything on the other side becomes more difficult.

The doorway effect also occurs when subjects take a walk through a *virtual* doorway.

HUMAN SEE, HUMAN DO. Why do we flinch in sympathy when we see someone stub her toe? Or cringe as we watch somebody smell sour milk? The answer is mirror neurons. These motor command neurons in the prefrontal cortex fire when we perform intentional actions, for example, picking up the milk carton to take a whiff. But a subset of these neurons fires when we watch *other* people perform the same action, creating something like a virtual-reality simulation in our minds. The signal is just strong enough for us to empathize with the person we're watching. Mirror neurons let us feel empathy by adopting another person's point of view and may also allow us to emulate behaviors and learn language. Because mirror neurons helped human beings become complex social animals, famed neuroscientist V. S. Ramachandran has called them the "basis of civilization."

In a study published in *Nature Neuroscience* called "Action Anticipation and Motor Resonance in Elite Basketball Players," a team of Italian neuroscientists showed clips of a player shooting free throws to three groups: Italian pro basketball players, coaches, and sportswriters. All three groups could predict the shot's outcome once they saw the arc of the ball. But only the athletes could call the shot *before* the ball left the player's hand. This suggests that to achieve excellence in a particular sport, players develop mirror neuron pathways to the point that they can accurately anticipate other players' actions.

STRONG
EMOTIONS CAN
BACKFIRE.

One way is through "empathy avoidance," which kicks in when you change the channel during an ASPCA commercial, for example. Singer Sarah McLachlan, who appeared in these famously tear-jerking spots, has said even she grabs the remote when her commercial comes on.

Imagine the plight of a girl fleeing a war-torn country. Okay, now try to imagine the plight of millions of refugees. Not as easy, was it? As our ability to offer meaningful help declines, so does our capacity for empathy. This psychological effect is called "compassion collapse."

Psychology professor Paul Bloom believes empathy is overrated in world leaders. Although he acknowledges empathy as a potential motivator to help and do good, Bloom also says it can be used to manipulate people. The best leaders, he argues, solve the world's problems by performing cost-benefit analyses and having a "certain enlightened aloofness."

―――――

Psychopaths are believed to be antisocial, lack empathy, and exhibit poor behavior control. Then again, that could describe some supposedly normal people. How can you tell if someone's an actual psychopath? Walk up behind her and make a loud noise. Or watch how she reacts when you yawn. Psychopaths don't startle easily, and they're immune to contagious yawning.

The Milgram shock experiment, first performed in 1961, explored the relationship between obedience and authority. In it, 65 percent of participants administered the highest possible voltage of electric shock when told to do so, even though they believed it caused their fellow participants tremendous pain. The experiment has been repeated many times across cultures to similar results.

The **Stanford prison experiment** of 1971 attempted to understand the psychological effects of being a prisoner versus being a guard. On its second day, students playing the part of prisoners staged a revolt. To restore order, student guards doled out what amounted to psychological torture, which many prisoners passively accepted. Some even harassed their fellow prisoners at the guards' request. With abuse spiraling out of control, the experiment was called off after six days.

In the aftermath of Dr. Martin Luther King Jr.'s assassination, third-grade teacher Jane Elliott conducted an empathy exercise not unlike the Stanford prison experiment. To the blue-eyed children in her class, she gave such privileges as second helpings at lunch, access to the new jungle gym, and five extra minutes at recess, and she encouraged them to play only with other blue-eyed kids. Children with brown eyes weren't allowed to drink from the same water fountain as the others and were singled out whenever they failed to follow the rules. The blue-eyed children grew arrogant and scored highly on tests, while the brown-eyed children became timid and scored poorly. When Elliott reversed the roles by giving privileges to the brown-eyed kids, the effects of the exercise sank in, and the taunts were less intense.

EMOTIONAL INTELLIGENCE IS ESSEN-
TIAL TO ALL OTHER INTELLIGENCE.
Getting along with other people is a precondition
for cognitive development, because the neural
pathways that deal with stress and handling
emotions are also used for learning.

———

As infants, boys are more emotionally
expressive than girls. According to Ronald
Levant, former president of the American
Psychological Association and a leading expert
on male psychology, this changes as children
grow older, because "it's stamped out of males,
and it's done by shame and punishment."

In the weeks immediately after the birth of a child, the father's testosterone levels drop by around 30 percent. Testosterone-deprived men are less likely to wander off in search of new mates to inseminate. They are also less aggressive, which is useful when there's a baby around.

Recent studies have revealed that bilingual children possess better problem-solving and social skills than children who speak only one language. From a very early age, bilingual kids learn how to interpret what's being asked of them, depending on who's asking.

TALK TO YOUR KIDS. A groundbreaking study called "The Early Catastrophe," published in *American Educator*, showed that a three-year-old's vocabulary, speech pattern, average number of words used, and conversation duration is 90 percent modeled on parental behavior. To wit: The vocabulary gap between kids whose parents spoke to them a lot and those whose parents didn't ran up to 30 million words! The research also demonstrated that vocabulary at age three can predict language skill at age 10.

———

The word *emotion* comes from the Middle French *émouvoir*, meaning "to stir up."

According to social psychologist Clay Routledge, nostalgia is a positive social emotion that promotes psychological health and well-being. Feeling sad? Crank up a cherished song from your childhood or look at old photographs. Routledge's research shows that even though nostalgia is often triggered by loneliness, it boosts our mood and strengthens our self-esteem, as well as boosting energy, inspiration, and optimism about the future.

A recent study indicates that nostalgia, a provider of psychological comfort, can also help create physical comfort. The multipart investigation revealed that nostalgia can be triggered by cold temperatures! Nostalgia brought on by listening to music was shown to increase body heat.

In 1688, Swiss medical student Johannes Hofer coined the term *nostalgia*—from the Greek *algos*, meaning "pain," and *nostos*, meaning "homecoming"—to describe the sometimes fatal homesickness afflicting Swiss mercenaries fighting in foreign wars. Hofer thought it was caused by the

vibration of "animal spirits" in the brain.
Other doctors thought it resulted
from brain damage caused by the
nonstop clanging of cowbells in the Swiss Alps.
The modern usage as a sentimental longing or
wistful affection for the past can be dated to 1920.

In 2015, neuroscientist Josh McDermott and a team at MIT located a neural pathway dedicated solely to music. In their study, control sounds from songbirds, car horns, flushing toilets, and barking dogs did not activate the pathway. But certain neurons displayed "music selectivity" and lit up when music was played. "To the extent that music functions for communication, it's quite different from [the specificity of] language," according to McDermott, a former club DJ. "But it obviously expresses something, typically something emotional."

In 2006, Italian cardiologist Luciano Bernardi set out to prove that listening to music lowers heart rate and blood pressure. He exposed subjects to a variety of music—from techno to Beethoven to the Red Hot Chili Peppers—with a two-minute period of silence in the middle of the sequence. He discovered that tempo, not genre, had the largest effect on heart rate. Fast music increased it, and slow music brought it down. But the real surprise came from the silence between songs, which proved far more relaxing than the most relaxing music. Concentrating (on music, in this instance) and then releasing your concentration creates a deeply relaxed state, similar to that of transcendental meditation.

The more we encounter a stimulus, the more we like it. Studies conducted by Robert Zajonc in the late 1960s confirmed that mere exposure creates a positive bias toward a stimulus. The "mere-exposure effect" explains why you find yourself happily humming a song you *hated* the first time you heard it.

More recent studies show that prolonged exposure takes us past a boredom threshold and actually reverses the mere-exposure effect. I *knew* I hated that song!

A common type of auditory hallucination involves hearing music in your head that isn't coming from any outside source. In his best-selling book *Hallucinations,* neurologist Oliver Sacks relates the case of a terrified Jewish patient who hallucinated the sounds of Nazi marching songs he had heard as a child in 1930s Germany.

We call songs that get stuck in our heads "earworms." Psychologists refer to them as "involuntary musical imagery," and a 2011 study published in *Psychology of Music* ascribed four primary triggers to the phenomenon: repeated exposure to the music; memory recalls; the emotion you're feeling at the time (called your "affective state"); and simply a wandering mind. The author of the study, music psychologist Victoria Williamson, suggests that focusing on a task can kill earworms. A rival theory advises chewing gum.

The **"propinquity effect"** is the mere-exposure effect applied to social situations. In other words, we become friends with people in terms of spatial or functional proximity. In one study, residents of an apartment building were four times more likely to have close friends living right next door than down the hall. Those living in an apartment at the bottom of the stairs had more friendships with people on higher floors than their first-floor neighbors did, simply because they ran into them more frequently.

THE WHOLE IS *OTHER* THAN THE SUM OF ITS PARTS. This expression, usually misquoted as "The whole is greater than the sum of its parts," comes from pioneering Gestalt psychologist Kurt Koffka. *Gestalt* is German for "shape" or "form," and Gestalt psychology posits that we perceive the whole image before identifying its parts. When we see a picture of a dog, for example, we don't look at the wagging tail, the pointy ears, the snout, and the furry coat, then say, "Oh, it's a dog!" We perceive the pooch in its entirety.

DOGS **REALLY DO RESEMBLE THEIR OWNERS.** A 2013 study published in *Anthrozoös*, a journal exploring the interactions between people and animals, showed that the perception of resemblance stems from similarities in the eyes. Weirder, perhaps, another paper, entitled "Not Only Dogs Resemble Their Owners, Cars Do, Too," showed that participants could match head-on grille shots of cars to their owners. Weirder even still, each car also resembled the owner's dog, though this transitive phenomenon worked only with purebreds.

Widely known for his experiments in classical conditioning, Ivan Pavlov was by training a physiologist primarily interested in digestion; he stumbled upon his behavioral insights almost by accident. Pavlov was a meticulous man who kept a strict schedule, which included feeding his laboratory dogs at precisely the same time every day. Before long he noticed they would begin to salivate the moment he entered the lab.

———

Pavlov discovered that dogs can be conditioned to respond to all sorts of neutral stimuli (bells, whistles, tuning forks, metronomes, etc.) when they are paired with a conditioned stimulus, e.g., food. Once the association is made, the neutral stimulus can be presented without the food, and the dog will still salivate. We now refer to this as a Pavlovian response.

In 1920, American behavioral psychologist
John B. Watson applied Pavlovian conditioning
to a nine-month-old boy. The Little Albert experiment, published in the *Journal of Experimental
Psychology,* is one of the most famous—and unethical—psychological case studies ever
conducted. Watson wanted to see if he could
condition an emotionally fearful response from a
seemingly normal child. He exposed Little Albert
to numerous neutral stimuli, including a dog, a
monkey, and a white rat. Albert showed no fear
and was particularly curious about the rat.
Watson then reintroduced the rodent but simultaneously clanged on a pipe. Like Pavlov's dogs,
Albert quickly associated the clanging with the rat
and cried whenever it was presented to him without the associated sound. Further experiments
found that Albert generalized his fearful response
to other white, furry objects as well.

If you've ever given your kid a time-out or used bacon to train your dog to sit, you've employed the radical behaviorism of B. F. Skinner. What we do is determined not by conscious choice, Skinner argued, but by reward and punishment. In other words, we repeat actions with good consequences and avoid actions with bad ones. Skinner called this "operant conditioning" and developed the Skinner box, containing levers an animal could press to dispense rewards (or punishments).

In 1954, neuroscientists James Olds and Peter Milner implanted electrodes into the septal regions of lab rats' brains and stuck them in a Skinner box. Every time a rat pressed the lever, the electrode shot a jolt directly into the pleasure center of its brain. Some rats hit the lever up to 7,000 times per hour, to the exclusion of all other activities. Self-stimulating male rats ignored females in heat and even tolerated shocks from an electrified floor to get at the lever. Female rats abandoned their young. Olds and Milner ultimately unhooked the rats to prevent them from starving to death.

When **not** conducting experiments in the lab, Skinner and his associates trained animals. He taught his children's cat to play the piano and the family beagle to play hide-and-go-seek; his colleagues got a pig to turn on a TV set, put dirty clothes in a hamper, and run a vacuum cleaner over the floor. After the attack on Pearl Harbor, the National Defense Research Committee allocated $25,000 (more than $400,000 today) to Project Pigeon, Skinner's idea to train pigeons to guide missiles toward enemy targets. The plan called for up to three pigeons to be stationed at a screen in the nose cone. When the birds saw a speck on the screen, they'd peck at it, thus steering the missile toward the target. Skinner succeeded in conditioning the pigeons to reliably peck at a screen up to 10,000 times in 45 minutes, but the fledgling project ultimately flagged.

After September 11, 2001, the CIA claimed experimental psychology justified its torture of suspected terrorists. One such technique involved inducing a state of "learned helplessness," which psychologists believed would encourage suspects to cooperate and thus escape feelings of depression. Psychologists now believe this technique resembles Pavlov's theories of aversive conditioning or avoidance learning, which he tested on dogs.

Dieters who try to suppress their thoughts about food often experience a vicious rebound effect. According to a 2010 study published in *Science,* called "Thought for Food: Imagined Consumption Reduces Actual Consumption," the key is to imagine yourself eating. Multiple experiments showed that people who imagined eating a particular food consumed less of it when given the chance.

In **"Winter Notes** on Summer Impressions," Fyodor Dostoevsky writes, "Try to pose for yourself this task: not to think of a polar bear, and you will see that the cursed thing will come to mind every minute." Daniel Wegner read this and figured thought suppression would be a good premise to test in his social psychology lab. He went on to introduce the "rebound effect," the idea that the more we try not to do something, the more we end up doing it. According to Wegner's theory of "ironic processes," when we try not to think of something, one part of our brain does this quite well, but another part checks in to make sure we're *not* thinking of that thing and, ironically, brings it up again!

Psychology **is** the study of the workings of the animal brain. Or is it? Researchers have found that plants know that they're being eaten.

———

HEALTH FOOD IS CONTRIBUTING TO THE OBESITY EPIDEMIC. In a study published in the *Journal of the Association for Consumer Research,* investigators confirmed consumer biases about healthy food being less filling. When a food was promoted as healthy, subjects reported being less full, ordered greater portions, and consumed more.

Evolutionary biologists believe our bitter taste receptors warn us away from substances that may be poisonous. Columbia University biologist Charles Zuker, who researches taste receptors, believes our fondness for bitter foods such as coffee and dark chocolate comes from a search for novelty and danger.

———

A study from the Harvard School of Public Health showed that adults who drank two to four cups of caffeinated coffee per day were half as likely to commit suicide as those who drank decaf. Caffeine creates that java jolt by blocking the brain's receptors for adenosine, a chemical that soothes the nervous system, and by spurring the release of more dopamine and glutamate, the brain's stimulants.

BEST. **BRUNCH. EVER.** Taking a picture of your food before eating, including the ritualistic act of composing your meal in the best possible light, can actually make food taste better.

In fact, any repeated, episodic, and fixed behavior—such as prayer or a particular way of carefully unwrapping a chocolate bar—can positively shift your perception of the food.

According to a Cornell Food and Brand Lab study, you're four times more likely to order dessert if your server is overweight. (You'll also order 17 percent more alcohol.) The server's body mass index, not anything the server says, sends out the social cue for a caloric splurge. And the skinnier the patron, the more pronounced the effect.

———

Obese people judge physical distances as greater than they really are. A 2016 study published in *Acta Psychologica* showed that our perception of distance is influenced by the overall energetic work needed to get there. Interestingly, beliefs about body size didn't affect distance perception; only actual body weight did.

Up to 80 percent of people never use their gym memberships. And around 90 percent of New Year's resolutions end in failure. What gives? The conventional wisdom is that lapses in willpower result from "ego depletion." Willpower is in short supply and decreases with overuse. Studies have shown that when ego depletion is high, you lose self-control even if you believe in unlimited willpower and are strongly motivated.

Ego depletion can also cause bad moods.

SELF-CONTROL
MAKES US
ANGRY.

In **"Grapes of Wrath,"** a cheekily titled paper published in the *Journal of Consumer Research,* subjects who exerted self-control by choosing an apple over a chocolate bar preferred to watch anger-themed movies and look at vexed faces, even expressing irritation at someone else's attempts to control their behavior.

A 2007 study found that showing subjects a desirable item for sale made part of their nucleus accumbens, home of the brain's pleasure center, light up in direct proportion to how much they wanted it. Revealing the item's price set off a "hedonic competition between the immediate pleasure of acquisition and an equally immediate pain of paying." This phenomenon partly explains the success of "fast fashion" chains such as Zara and H&M, whose low prices effectively remove the pain point of committing to something trendy that you want.

Many shoppers admit they are "addicted" to fast fashion, despite knowing that the industry's low prices are often driven by unethical practices such as child labor.

Pica **is** a mental disorder involving the persistent consumption of substances containing no nutritional value. It gets its name from the magpie (whose Latin name is *Pica*), a bird notorious for eating just about anything. Doctors have removed blockages of chalk, sand, dirt, drywall, metal, grass, burnt matches, coffee grounds, stones, paint chips, and even mothballs from pica sufferers. It is most common among children, but some pregnant women also display pica symptoms.

Tourette syndrome is an inherited neuro-psychiatric disorder manifesting in recognizable physical tics and, sometimes, coprolalia, or socially inappropriate outbursts. Although the exact causes are unknown, music may help bring the tics and verbal impulses under control.

As a medical student in France, Georges Gilles de la Tourette was interested in hysteria and mesmerism. In 1881, he translated a study by American neurologist George Miller Beard documenting an unusually extreme startle response among a handful of French Canadian lumberjacks in New England. When startled, the afflicted would jump, scream, flail their arms, or throw objects. Jumping Frenchmen of Maine syndrome is an extraordinarily rare disorder, and its cause is unknown.

According to a 2016 study, Henry VIII probably had chronic traumatic encephalopathy (CTE), a progressive degenerative disease common among football players and others who suffer repeated blows to the head. Historians generally agree that young Henry was affable, athletic, and a wise strategist. But in his 30s, he experienced several concussions while jousting, one of which left him unconscious for two hours. CTE would explain Henry's famous memory loss, explosive anger, iffy impulse control, depression, headaches, insomnia, and even his impotence.

Use of the word *sex* to mean "intercourse," rather than "gender," is often attributed to comedian Mae West and her 1926 play entitled, well, *Sex*. In 1949, a year after sexologist Alfred Kinsey published his landmark study *Sexual Behavior in the Human Male*, West remarked that the good doctor "makes it easy for me. Now I don't have to draw 'em any blueprints."

———

POSTCOITAL POSTS? Tweeting, texting, and posting on Facebook have replaced the postcoital cigarette. According to a 2009 survey, 36 percent of people under 35 check social media sites after having sex.

A 2015 study published in *The Journal of Sex Research* analyzed 35 years of data from the General Social Survey, a database of American attitudes taken from annual polls. The study's findings contradicted claims that watching pornography leads to negative attitudes toward women. In fact, the data set from more than 28,000 people showed that porn viewers were more likely to see women as equals than porn abstainers. Heavy watchers of porn also had more positive attitudes about women holding high positions in public office.

A 2011 study published in the *Journal of Social, Evolutionary, and Cultural Psychology* found no empirical evidence that men fall asleep first after having sex with women. The study did show, however, that participants whose partners habitually fell asleep first had a much higher need for expressions of emotional bonding and affection after sex. Through the lens of evolutionary psychology, falling asleep first after sex is an unconscious way of postponing conversations about commitment.

DUELING **PSYCHOLOGISTS.** In 1899, Sigmund Freud introduced his theory of the Oedipus complex, which describes a child's sexual desire for its parent. Freud applied this formula to both boys and girls, but Oedipus complexes more often refer to a son's attraction to his mother. This left an opening for Carl Jung, who in 1913 countered with the Electra complex, a conflict in which a daughter feels psychosexual competition with her mother for the father's favors. Freud apparently despised Jung's term.

———

Because their brains are more complex, women need more sleep than men.

Nearly one in five college students suffers from exploding head syndrome, according to a 2015 study published in the *Journal of Sleep Research*. EHS is a psychological disorder in which a hallucinated sound—a loud bell, say, or a gunshot—suddenly wakes you up. Usually, your brain powers down incrementally once you fall asleep. But brain monitoring of EHS patients showed a delay in shutting down some areas, followed by a burst of neural activity where sound is processed.

A **2016 study** of 91 people who had experienced traumatic events established a direct link between nightmares and suicidal behavior. Published in the *Journal of Clinical Sleep Medicine,* the research found nightmares acted as a stressor, reinforcing feelings of defeat, entrapment, and hopelessness.

———————

BAD THINGS HAPPEN WHEN YOU DON'T GET ENOUGH SLEEP. Studies have shown that being awake for 17 hours straight had the same effect on performance as a blood alcohol level of 0.5. Poor judgment caused by sleep deprivation has resulted in nuclear leaks at Three Mile Island and Chernobyl, the *Exxon Valdez* oil spill, and the *Challenger* explosion, among many other catastrophes.

Stress wakes you up in the morning. The "natural alarm clock" some people claim to have is just a burst of adrenocorticotropin, a stress hormone secreted by the anterior pituitary gland. When you rise before your alarm goes off, you're unconsciously anticipating the stress of waking up.

YOU CAN'T
TICKLE YOURSELF
WHEN YOU'RE
AWAKE.

Nor can you tickle yourself in your dreams. You can't even tickle yourself if you're having an out-of-body experience. When your brain fires off an action command to move a limb, for example, it soon sends out a shadow signal, called a corollary discharge, which predicts your movement and dampens your senses. It's one way a healthy brain helps you create a sense of self and distinguish your internal experience of the world from external stimuli.

Schizophrenics, however, *can* tickle themselves.

Milton Rokeach's 1964 case study *The Three Christs of Ypsilanti* chronicles three paranoid schizophrenic men, each of whom believed he was Jesus Christ. Rokeach had them transferred to Ypsilanti State Hospital in Michigan, predicting that confronting one another (i.e., other incarnations of God's one and only son) would force the men to abandon their delusions. Though their conflicts gradually diminished, the Christs plunged deeper into their psychoses. Rokeach later admitted the two-year experiment cured only his own "godlike delusion that I could manipulate them out of their beliefs."

If you're born with cortical blindness—i.e., blindness caused by damage to the brain, rather than the eyes—you can't develop schizophrenia.

Scientists have built a schizophrenic computer. They did it by teaching a computer first-person stories about everyday things, along with third-person stories that were more like action movies, including some terrorist plots. After trying the experiment at speeds approximating the workings of the human brain, the scientists programmed the computer to understand and retell the stories at a hyperaccelerated rate. The machine began to mix them up and even claimed to be the terrorist who had planted a bomb.

Dan McAdams, a psychologist who specializes in the autobiographical self, argues that by the age of two we recognize ourselves as actors in our own stories. By eight, we become agents in those stories. And by early adulthood, we think of ourselves as the authors.

In a study published in *Proceedings of the National Academy of Sciences,* researchers swayed nearly 50 percent of participants who were undecided about a political election by programming search engines to display a positive article about one candidate as the highest-ranking result. By providing positive articles about the opposing candidate only in lower search results, the researchers were able to manipulate unsuspecting participants. The ramifications of this experiment are astonishing. The top two results of a search term get half the total traffic; the top 10 results get more than 90 percent. If Google, the world's most popular search engine, rigged its results, users probably wouldn't even notice.

A **report** entitled "The Many Faces of Lies" describes a study in which participants were asked to keep track of every time they intentionally tried to mislead someone. The results revealed that they told about one or two lies per day—about the same number of times you hit the fridge for a snack. Perhaps not surprisingly, one out of every two conversations between a college student and her mother contained a lie.

BUT ENOUGH ABOUT ME, LET'S TALK ABOUT ME.

We like to talk about ourselves. Brain scans show that bragging stimulates regions belonging to the mesolimbic dopamine system, part of the pleasure and reward pathway that drives our desires for money, food, and sex. A 2012 study published in *Proceedings of the National Academy of Sciences* showed that people were even willing to forgo small amounts of money just so they could talk about themselves.

———

Extroverts may *think* they make the best salespeople, but they're wrong. According to a study published in *Psychological Science,* introverts sell just as well as extroverts. In fact, the most effective sellers are ambiverts, people who are in the middle of the introvert-extrovert spectrum. Ambiverts can muster just enough enthusiasm to close a sale but are also good at listening to customers and not being overconfident.

By reputation, narcissists have an unhealthy sense of entitlement. They're arrogant. They have an inflated idea of their own importance. They lack empathy and are poor interpersonal communicators. Who wants to hang out with anyone like that? According to the study "Narcissists of a Feather Flock Together," the answer is other narcissists.

A series of three studies published in *Social Psychological and Personality Science* revealed that conspiracy theory believers are often narcissists with low self-esteem.

RED FACT, BLUE FACT. Political beliefs make you stupid—or at least bad at basic math. A 2013 study led by Yale law professor Dan Kahan showed that people with better than average math skills failed to do simple arithmetic problems when the data conflicted with their political beliefs. The study provided Democrats and Republicans with a set of data and required them to do simple math to gauge the efficacy of gun control. When Democrats examined data showing that gun control made crime rise, they got the problem wrong more than half the time. Republicans fared even worse. Only 20 percent of Republicans who looked at data proving gun control lowered crime got the math right.

The implicit association test measures how quickly we make associations with words flashed on a screen. Studies have shown that political partisans were quicker to assign positive attributes to someone in their own party than to a member of a competing party. Soccer fans needed more time to associate a positive word with their archrivals. And white people, even those who said they weren't racist, took longer to associate black people with positive attributes than they did other whites.

Liberals **and conservatives** favor different problem-solving strategies. In a study at Northwestern University, participants who identified as either liberal or conservative were given a series of nonpolitical word problems and then asked how they solved them. While conservatives used intuitive insight and logical analysis more or less interchangeably, liberals favored insight over analysis by a factor of nearly two to one.

In his best-selling book *Descartes' Error,*
neurologist Antonio Damasio describes a
patient he calls Elliot, whose frontal lobe was
damaged when he had a brain tumor removed.
After the operation, Elliot performed well on
IQ tests, long- and short-term memory tests,
and various math problems. But further tests
revealed Elliot had lost his ability to feel
emotion. He also became indecisive about
personal and social matters. When asked to
choose between two restaurants, he could
perform a cost-benefit analysis—comparing
menus, atmosphere, customer traffic—but he
couldn't *decide.* Damasio's work showed that
assigning emotional value is a precondition
for reasoning. Thus, Elliot's decision-making
landscape was, according to the author,
"hopelessly flat."

BOREDOM IS SO HOT RIGHT NOW.

In a 2003 survey, U.S. teenagers who admitted to being bored were 50 percent more likely than their peers to take up smoking, drinking, or illegal drugs. Boredom is one of the top triggers for binge eating. And, in another study, many participants gave themselves small electric shocks rather than be left alone with their thoughts.

There are two kinds of boredom: "state boredom" and "trait boredom." The former is being bored in the moment; the latter is being routinely bored by what you're doing, no matter what it is.

According to the Minnesota Multiphasic
Personality Inventory, administered to high
school and college students since 1945, kids
have been feeling increasingly more anxious
and depressed for more than 70 years.

———————

For millennia, religious leaders have conten-
ded that burning incense is good for the soul.
Psychologists now believe it's also good for the
mind. Research shows that burning frankincense—
resin from trees in the genus *Boswellia*—activates
ion channels in the brain to alleviate anxiety and
depression.

WTF [psychology]

The **"halo effect,"** first described by
American psychologist Edward Thorndike
in his 1920 paper "A Constant Error in
Psychological Ratings," is a confirmation bias
whereby we judge people with one positive
trait to have other positive traits, even when
confronted with evidence to the contrary.
Thorndike asked military commanding officers
to evaluate their soldiers based on numerous
qualities and found the officers judged their
men holistically—that is, they were either good
across the board or completely useless.

Further research implicates the halo effect in our unconscious desire to reinforce our first impressions. The old adage about them rings true: Once made, first impressions are very hard to change. That's because they're based in snap decisions ruled by the "affect heuristic," a mental shortcut that sums up all the information available in that first moment—how someone is dressed, how they smell, whether they have good posture, etc.—and renders a quick, pleasant feeling, in the case of a positive experience, before we can even think about it. First impressions are also deeply rooted in our emotions. When people talk about having a gut feeling, they're talking about the affect heuristic.

Once an angel, always an angel. Numerous studies have shown that beautiful people are the greatest beneficiaries of a strong halo effect. The rest of us assume good-looking people are more intelligent, talented, kind, and honest than they really may be.

———

Once a devil, always a devil. Overweight people, for example, may experience the horns effect, the opposite of the halo effect, when they are stereotyped as lazy.

WE AIM TO KILL. Splashback is the technical term for urine that splashes out of men's urinals and onto the floor or walls. It's the bane of every maintenance person who has to mop it up and anyone who shares a home with an inattentive man or boy. But in the early 1990s, Jos van Bedaf, a manager in the custodial department at Amsterdam's Schiphol Airport, had the idea to place a decal depicting a fly in the urinals, for target practice. The result? According to Klaus Reichardt, inventor of the waterless urinal, *half* as much splashback—some claim a reduction as high as 80 percent. The fly is particularly effective because males think of it as unsanitary and unconsciously believe a stream of pee can kill it.

SINS OF THE FATHER. A phobia is just an extreme and irrational aversion to something, right? Maybe not. A study published in *Nature Neuroscience* showed that phobias can change aspects of our DNA—and we can pass these changes on to our children. To demonstrate this, researchers trained mice to fear the smell of cherry blossoms before allowing them to breed. When the young mice encountered cherry blossoms for the first time, they exhibited fear. The team later examined the offspring's brains and found structural changes in areas responsible for odor detection.

Hermann Rorschach's nickname as a child was Klecks, which is German for "inkblot." Growing up in Switzerland, Rorschach played at klecksography, a popular childhood game of making pictures out of inkblots. He developed his Rorschach inkblot test to examine personality and thought processes.

Stendhal syndrome is named after the French novelist who succumbed to fainting spells upon entering Florence's Basilica of Santa Croce. "I was in a sort of ecstasy, from the idea of being in Florence," Stendhal wrote. "Life was drained from me. I walked with the fear of falling." Although hundreds of cases have been documented in Florence alone, Stendhal syndrome is considered a psychosomatic disorder, meaning it's all in the sufferers' heads.

DO YOU SEE WHAT I'M SAYING? What you see influences what you hear. But when the two don't match, you experience a perceptual illusion known as the McGurk effect. In their paper "Hearing Lips and Seeing Voices," Harry McGurk and John MacDonald demonstrate that subjects who listened to a recording of someone saying "ba" while watching a video of someone mouthing "ga" heard neither. Instead, their brains combined the two stimuli so they heard "da." The McGurk effect works even when you're aware of the phenomenon!

LEMONS ARE FAST. PRUNES ARE SLOW.

These **statements** don't have any intrinsic meaning. Yet when people are asked about the relative speed of lemons and prunes, they overwhelmingly give the same answer. Most people also believe that boulders are sour and that red is heavier than yellow.

Synesthesia **is** a neurological condition in which two or more senses are coupled, with one sense input creating an involuntary connection to another. Synesthetes may, for example, "see" sounds, "taste" colors, or "feel" flavors. In a case study discussed in *Scientific American*, neuroscientists V. S. Ramachandran and Edward Hubbard describe a color-blind synesthete who "sees" hues when he looks at numbers. This grapheme-color synesthesia can be caused by cross-activation, since the neural regions for processing letters and numbers lie adjacent to those for color.

Do shapes have sounds? In 2001, V. S. Ramachandran and Edward Hubbard showed subjects a rounded form and an angular one, then asked which was "kiki" and which was "bouba." The results were nearly unanimous: The rounded shape was bouba, and the angular one was kiki. Why do we *know* this? Psychologists describe this phenomenon as "crossmodal perception," in which two or more of our senses share an association.

Graphic designer Sarah Hyndman, author of *Why Fonts Matter,* asked women to choose the typeface they'd most like to date. From a field of nine candidates, a plurality chose Franklin Gothic bold condensed. A sans serif type designed by Morris Fuller Benton in the early 1900s, Franklin Gothic has a strong, reliable, and distinctly American character. Hyndman believes our brains attach meaning to different letter shapes (people just want to be friends with Helvetica, she says). This helps explain the results of another experiment she conducted, in which jelly beans tasted either sweet or sour depending on the font of the "Eat Me" sign.

In 2012, documentary filmmaker Errol Morris conducted an unscientific poll in *The New York Times* entitled "Are You an Optimist or a Pessimist?" Morris's quiz set out not to test people's philosophical temperaments, however, but the trustworthiness of various typefaces. The font that readers thought contained the most truth was Baskerville. The least trustworthy typeface? Comic Sans.

That's pathetic. *Pathetic fallacy* is a literary term referring to the personification of inanimate objects or entities that lack consciousness. Despite such chestnuts as "Nature abhors a vacuum," pathetic fallacy is discouraged in science writing, as it can encourage sentimentalism, psychological projection, and magical thinking.

———

In Thailand you can buy dolls known as *luk thep* ("child angels"), which increasing numbers of people believe will bring them good fortune. To animate their dolls with a spirit, owners have monks conduct an anointing ceremony, called *plook sek*. Owners then treat the dolls to meals at restaurants, jewelry, and, in some cases, their own seats on airplanes.

In his book *The Luck Factor*, psychologist Richard Wiseman recounts having study participants identify themselves as either lucky or unlucky before he placed a newspaper in front of them. He then asked them to count the number of photographs inside. The unlucky people took about two minutes to perform the task, the lucky ones just a few seconds. How was this possible? Wiseman had inserted a half-page advertisement on the second page, which read, "Stop counting—there are 43 photographs in this newspaper." The unlucky people didn't see it.

———

Wiseman contends that we create our own luck through the ways we think and behave. "Lucky" people have a positive attitude, are more resilient, and listen to their intuition, which allows them to see chance opportunities.

MIT **professor** Richard Larson is an expert
in queuing theory, the mathematical study of
waiting in lines. By his estimate, Americans spend
roughly 37 billion hours a year in lines, and the
waits can waste up to two years of their lives.
What's worse, it *feels* even longer. According to
Larson, occupied time—when we're engaged in
activities we care about—feels shorter than the
unoccupied time we spend standing in line. What
to do? Experts say choose the line on the left.
Since the vast majority of us are right-handed,
we unconsciously tend to move to the right.

A couple of Danish economists demonstrated that the best way to cut wait times is to abolish the standard first-come, first-served system, which incentivizes people to show up early to secure a good spot in line. They proposed a *last*-come, first-served system, because it incentivizes people to stay away. Subjects in their experiment tended to get in

line at staggered times, thus cutting the wait.
When the researchers asked if people would
be willing to implement this system, however,
the answer was an emphatic no. This strong
emotional reaction against a more efficient
but seemingly unfair practice isn't surprising.
Fairness is processed in the anterior insular
cortex, the seat of our emotional reactions.

Our **brains** are hardwired to rebuke unfair behavior. In an "ultimatum game" scenario, researchers gave one player a small amount of money to split with a second player. If both agreed on the split, they could keep their shares, but if the second player refused the offer, both players would get nothing. Neuroimaging studies show that the anterior insular cortex lights up when we receive unfair offers. So even though we know two bucks is better than nothing, we'll reject lowball bids outright.

The next time you negotiate, offer your interlocutor a cushy chair and a warm beverage, then sit in a hard, rigid chair. A 2008 study published in *Science* affirmed that participants holding a warm mug judged others as having warmer personalities than did those who held a cold beverage. A 2010 study, also published in *Science,* showed that people sitting in wooden chairs negotiated harder with car dealers and got a better deal. The chair's hardness produced an unconscious demonstration of rigid thinking.

Daniel Kahneman, winner of the Nobel Prize in Economics, says we feel and fear loss much more than we enjoy gain. "People aren't concerned about their level of wealth," he determined, "but about changes in their wealth."

———

You've finally decided what you want to do with your life, and you're so excited you want to tell the world! Don't. The positive feeling you get from sharing your plans tricks your mind into thinking you've already accomplished them. Kurt Lewin, widely regarded as the father of social psychology, conducted studies in the 1920s showing that your brain can substitute thinking for doing. More recent studies by NYU psychology professor Peter Gollwitzer showed that sharing intentions created a premature sense of completeness that sapped participants' motivation.

Evolutionary psychologists speculate that Stockholm syndrome, expressed when hostages empathize with and begin to have positive feelings for their captors, may have evolved from the days when our hunter-gatherer ancestors routinely abducted members of another tribe, particularly women. Abductees who resisted capture risked getting killed on the spot.

Autism spectrum disorder (ASD) is a complex brain development condition that affects social interactions, behavior, and communication skills. Currently, no medical test exists for ASD, so psychologists must perform specific behavioral evaluations. But because the doctors are looking at *social* behaviors, children generally can't be diagnosed with accuracy until they're at least two years old.

Researchers at the Weizmann Institute of Science in Israel developed a sniff test that may help diagnose ASD much earlier. A 2015 paper published in *Current Biology* explains that children usually modulate how they sniff various odors—for example, they'll take a deep sniff of flowers and a shallow one of rotting fish. But children with ASD do not modulate their sniffs. The more severe the ASD symptoms, researchers found, the deeper the kids sniffed the unpleasant smells.

Because **schizophrenia** and autism may inhabit opposite ends of the diametric model of mental illness, one way to treat schizophrenics is to make them somewhat autistic.

———

Some **studies** suggest that one-third of people on the autism spectrum have perfect pitch.

In a French study, participants read a short story aloud while their voices were altered to sound happy, neutral, or sad. Unaware that their sounds were being manipulated, the participants shifted their moods to match the tone of their voices.

We overestimate how much other people share our opinions, attitudes, behaviors, and beliefs. This is called the "false consensus effect," most famously demonstrated in a social psychology experiment at Stanford University. Students were asked if they'd be willing to walk around campus for half an hour carrying a sandwich board that read "Eat at Joe's." Those who agreed believed about two-thirds of the other students would also agree. But those who declined likewise believed about two-thirds would decline. When asked to describe people in the remaining third, both groups characterized them as odd or deviant.

CURIOUSER AND CURIOUSER.

Alice in Wonderland syndrome is a neurological disorder in which the sufferer perceives
herself or nearby objects to be shrinking or growing in size, reminiscent of the title character's
experience in Lewis Carroll's *Alice's Adventures in
Wonderland.* The condition is rare, mostly affects
children, and is often described as a migraine
aura, a visual disturbance that can precede
migraine headaches. As we know from his jour-
nals, Carroll suffered from migraines, prompting
speculation that he had experienced the same
somatic strangeness as his literary heroine.

One **criticism** of Western psychological studies is that the participants are all WEIRD. That is, they're Western, educated, and from industrialized, rich, democratic countries— a combination of attributes that is by no means universal.